This book is dedicated to:

Kevin Gibbs	Valerie Cooper
George Cooper	Graham Parsons
Debbie Walker	Julie Parsons
Tina Hannay	Brian Parsons
Donald Gibbs	Sandra Gibbs
Shirley Tadd	Sharon Langley
Brendan Quinn	Tracy White
Tanya Lestrange	Margaret Morton
Pam Romboli	Lesley Gibbs
Pam Yeager Roper	Adrian Gibbs
Kathie Greenly Cox	Ann Osborn
Charlie-L Edwards	Jenny Merredew
Ajoy Dua	Aruna Dua
Helen Wright	Kim Edwards
Darren Halford	Russ Bradford
Steve Swainsbury	Tim Lockington
David Openshaw	Lynn Openshaw
Glynnis Gutteridge	Katy Osborn

Members of Parkinson's Road groups
and Parkinson's hero: Michael. J. Fox.

Contents

Part 3.

PART ONE

Before Diagnosis

Come with me. Let us jump back in time to the 1970's and 1980's. My great aunt Phyllis was a robust, funny and indomitable woman. She lived some way from where I grew up in West London and so I didn't get to see her outside of significant family events. I had spoken with her many times, by telephone, in my childhood and teenage years and I looked up to her as did, I believe, the whole family.

I had seen her at the funeral of her twin brother, my lovely, funny wonderful grandfather. His name was Wilfred but he was known to everyone as Bill. Phyllis was a woman of short stature but she had an energy about her that always made me think of the renowned Titanic sinking survivor, Molly Brown. This was due to the formidable strength of character, for which my great aunt was known. To my family, she was our very own 'Unsinkable Molly Brown'.

The last time that I saw my dear great aunt was in the 1980's and it was shocking. Gone was the embodiment of Molly Brown. Instead, my great aunt had become slight, frail and her once robust energy was diminished to being doddery and unstable.

Her emboldened voice, a mere whisper and her direct assertiveness reduced to floor gazing and uncertainty. The cause of this unthinkable change was Parkinson's Disease.

I did not know much about Parkinson's, but what I saw, in my great aunt, told me all I needed.

Upon her death, not very long after that visit, I found myself deeply saddened. I recognised that she had suffered years of deterioration and that her quiet dignity, whilst stoical, had kept her isolated from us as she increasingly declined. This once social whirlwind of a woman had become solitary and secluded, in so many ways.

I found peace in the idea that she was finally free of the shackles and hideous confines of Parkinson's. Though I knew little of the disease, back then, I could see how ravaged my great aunt was, by Parkinson's.

In some way, I drew comfort from imagining that the disease was laid to rest, too. This depleting blight on the well-being of my family was now gone. I could not have been more wrong.

Throughout my childhood and teenage years, I experienced mysterious symptoms. They were mysterious, simply because I did not know their cause and neither did any of the Doctor's we went to see. I was forever feeling ill; out of sorts and exhausted. I was full of life and fun one day and then I would have a day or two of weakness and exhaustion that would follow. I was forever finding ways to stay off school.

I actually loved my school friends, my teachers and my lessons, but I just so frequently felt that I had no energy or capacity to see a day through at school. I would experience pains, co-ordination difficulties and digestive system problems that were exacerbated by the anxiety that accompanied my difficulties.

By the time I reached sixteen years of age, I knew that something was just not right. Nobody that I knew, of my peer group, were experiencing the symptoms that I was experiencing. I believed that I had some sort of undiagnosed illness.

One day, having been at rest on the sofa with a cup of tea, I started to feel what I used to imagine as fireworks going off in my arms and hands. I became fidgety. I had a tingle of searing energy in my hands; a need to fidget and move. I would feel a tension along with this. Then, as it progressed, I would feel increasingly anxious.

I got up from the sofa, went to the kitchen to wash and dry my cup and to put it away. Our beautiful, protective Alsatian dog, Rebel, followed me into the kitchen.

It was a simple, every-day task and it would yet again end in disaster. It was the same as many times before. I had lifted the cup to put it back into the kitchen cupboard, where it belonged. As I started to release my grip on the cup, my hand started to cramp, my arm became tense and awkward as my bicep went into spasm and intense pain.

The cup fell to the floor and smashed into thousands of tiny pieces. Then ensued the mayhem of trying to get Rebel away from the tiny shards of china, some frantic sweeping and vacuuming of the floor. In the background, my mum fussed and tried to be helpful. My mum and I would approach this knowingly and yet somehow resigned to the reality of not knowing what was causing this.

At sixteen years of age these incidents were not frequent, by any means, but they were not uncommon. I had always thought that I was just clumsy and weak. Throughout childhood, I was the boy who would sometimes be ridiculously clumsy. I was the boy who would sometimes wake up and feel incredibly weak and unwell. I would suffer the most horrific and vivid nightmares. I was a frequent sleep-walker.

I suffered sudden digestive problems and, in an attempt to manage my own gut health, I was the boy who was vegetarian for long stretches at a time. I was the boy who stayed off school more than anyone else, because I was exhausted, in pain or struggling with numerous bizarre symptoms.

By age sixteen, I was the teen who had suffered with the most hideous migraines. These would sometimes last for days and the experience was excruciating.

My dad had left the family home when I was fourteen, so it was left to my mum to sit up with me all night, to bathe my head and to hold me as I screamed in agony or as I threw up repeatedly during these day of enduring migraines. To be fair, she had always been the one of my parents who would do this for me. She has been a truly amazing mother and she still is.

My dad would usually mutter about how he didn't understand it and blame my mum's side of the family. Ironically, I suspect he was right about the origins of my health problems being from my maternal line. He would generally be working away, in the film industry, so he was not as present for most of these events as he otherwise might have been.

He cared, hugely. They both did. My dad's method of coping, however, would always be to suggest throwing money at a problem. He seemed aloof to the idea of simply giving comfort to his somewhat worried, distressed son.

This was my normal. Doctors were perplexed. They would simply refer to that fact that I'd had numerous tests over the years of my childhood. So many small examples of me ending up in difficulty with my health. Too many to list. The medical profession seemed baffled. They went from suggesting Leukemia through to suggesting it was allergies, through to suggesting my health issues must be psychosomatic.

There was nothing we could do to find treatment for symptoms that seemed to affect different parts of me for varying periods of time. My parents and I knew that something was not right. We knew that I was suffering from some form of illness which seemed to affect my ability to co-ordinate my body, that affected my digestive health, that caused me pain and migraines and that left me experiencing varying degrees of exhaustion and emotional distress, as a result.

As time progressed, I started to believe that the psychosomatic aspect may have held some truth. I did not have a peaceful childhood, in spite of all of the fun and adventure that it involved. My family suffered a high number of losses

and the exhilarating. I practically grew up in the film and television studios at Pinewood, Shepperton and Ealing. I mixed with the famous and I was able to watch in wonder and awe as my dad worked on the biggest blockbuster movies of the late twentieth century.

I had great childhood friends in the street where I grew up and at school; many of whom remain friends to this day. We shared many exciting adventures and fun times and I look back at my childhood with great joy and gratitude.

My closest friend was from another culture. I grew up with the insight and values of the Hindu tradition, among those of my own family. I am truly grateful and enriched by what I learned from my friend, Ajoy, and his family.

I indulged in creativity, more sports than I can probably remember and life was generally good. My parents left me in no doubt that I was loved and that I could achieve anything I set my mind to, in life. I felt emboldened by all of this. I was also aware that I was privileged.

Until my dad left the family home, we had more money than most families around us and so I was fortunate in ways that I have never taken for granted. That said, life became very financially strained when my dad left and I learnt what it was to live with the threat of poverty over us.

I had to watch my mum work three jobs and near kill herself from the exhaustion she suffered to see me through school, to keep a roof over our heads, food on our table and to have some money for living. This was my normal. It was a childhood of extremes.

At the time, I decided that the pressure of going on in my studies, through to University, would not be a good idea. I felt that my poor mum would certainly die if she had to work any harder to sustain my studies and I felt that I wanted to give back to her.

I decided to quit school after one year of my A Level's. I quit school and got a job. I would return to study later in life.

One sunny afternoon, on a day in which I had again felt too unwell to attend school, I almost discovered the cause of my mystery illness. I was watching a soap opera on tv, though I cannot recall which one. One of the main characters started to experience symptoms that I recognised. She was dropping things. She had co-ordination problems. She would have sleep disturbances and there were her headaches. In fact, she was diagnosed, in the show, with Multiple Sclerosis.

I recall saying to my mum that I had seen this character's plight and that I wondered if I, too, might have MS? I recall saying that if it was not MS, then it must be something of a similar nature; something relating to my brain. A different neurological illness, perhaps?

My mum did what all caring parents do. She reassured me that I was fine and that if anything worrying developed further, we would go to the doctor and ask for yet more tests. Both my mum and I seemed, somehow, to have completely failed to remember the plight of great aunt Phyllis. This was a major disconnect and still baffles me.

It is true that we had only occasional contact with great aunt Phyllis. I can only suppose that we, like many people, fell into the idea that Parkinson's was only a disease of the elderly. As something rarely mentioned in the media or among people we knew, there was absolutely no knowledge about the existence of Young Onset Parkinson's Disease. It would never have entered our heads to even consider Parkinson's as a possible cause of my ills.

Further tests were not needed, it seemed. Life went on and I progressed into my mid-twenties with roughly the same level of occasional and varying symptoms. I had just started to believe that this was how I was and that there was no need to think any more of it. I concluded that I should simply manage the symptoms, if or when they flared up.

In fact, some of the symptoms eased down and could even be forgotten for a while. I literally forgot how bad some of the earlier years of my health difficulties had been. I believe that this was related to a renewed sense of relief and freedom from having had so many difficulties, health wise, early on. Being free of ailment, suddenly the opportunity to not have to think of health would have been second nature.

Life seemed to be getting better and, by my mid-twenties, I had met my future husband. Things seemed much more hopeful. I was generally only experiencing migraines by this point, as most other symptoms had diminished. I was going to be alright, after all. Again, I could not have been more wrong.

Origins

She was always loud on the phone.
Ever raucous and so beguiling.
Her sharp wit was dry as a stone.
A matriarch so mystifying.
She lived in an attic alone,
Below which, her son was residing.

I was shocked, that last time we met.
The memory of which still haunts me.
I thought I knew what to expect.
The sad image of her now reigns free.
In some ways I'd like to forget.
The last vestiges she came to be.

She had been vivacious and fun.
A presence commanding and yet bright.
Always active and on the run.

Then Parkinson's had dimmed down
her light.
Her effervescence now seemed done.
Her existence reduced to a plight.

She had heard us walk through the
door.
Without balance, she just could not rise.
She sullenly looked at the floor.
Where before she'd have looked in my
eyes.
Great Aunt had so much to endure.
The disease had diminished her size.

Unsure what to make of this scene,
To me Parkinson's was just a name.
If only the future was seen.
We'd have known that my fate is the
same.
So much could have been shared
between.
Together, we'd have felt far less shame.

Parkinson's road lies before me.
But my Great Aunt had walked this
road first.
With this baton now passed to me.
There are times when it feels I've been
cursed.
Yet our tree is strong and mighty.
Bring it on, Parkinson's, do your worst.

Signposting

The street in dark oblivion. Pitch.
Black. Silent. Save for a savvy street
cat. The house. Homely. Mum and
dad slouching downstairs. Sight on the
significant box.
The boy stirs in his slumber. Something
unstills him. He sits. He shifts. He
stands up. The steady downstairs
promenade. Slow. Strange.
Subconscious. Unconscious. Sleepy
steps.

Into the sitting room. Staring into
space. Steady pace. Suggests some
purpose.
Suspecting. Mum and Dad look up.
Their son suggests he supposedly seeks
something. Sweet boy. Just around
seven years of age. Sage for his age.
Such a sleepy soul. Onwards.

Somehow still walking. The dog sees.
Somehow the strange slumber still
persists.

He stretches. He seeks. In stealth he
starts for the door to the outside. The
garden. It is shut. Locked. Firmly. His
parents cease their observation. The
watching stops. They stand. They
shelter him. The say his name. They
surround him. They awaken him. The
boy stands and stares. He is startled.
For a moment. He smiles and says
sorry.

He had been sleepwalking yet again.
Lucid dreams. He safely returns to his
slumber. Years later. Diagnosed. He
believes. Sleepwalking. Lucid dreams.
Childhood symptoms.

Something is Happening

Something is happening.
That is becoming clear to me.
Is it life shattering?
For I'm just not how I should be.

My writing seems so small.
I find I'm cramping up a lot.
I feel as though I'll fall.
Temperature control is shot.

I can't co-ordinate.
So much crockery is broken.
I stay awake so late.
I'd sleep on, if not awoken.

I feel a lot of pain.
Did I mention constipation?
Fatigue hit me again.
This triggers my consternation.

I may often feel stressed.
My migraines are terrifying.
I struggle to get dressed.
I cannot get up from lying.

These symptoms come and go.
And, frankly, there are many more.
To the Doctors I go.
They must perceive me as a bore.

Perhaps it's in my head,
For there seems no consistency.
My Doctor must see red,
When each few months he hears from
me.

But it's all I can do.
These ailments are so impacting.
I just want an answer.
Clarity that is exacting.

I do not know the source.
This experience makes no sense.
So will I last the course?
Or will I fall at the next fence?

It's true that I am scared.
It really could be something bad.
Yet when I am prepared,
Real information makes me glad.

I monitor myself.
If this is happening to you,
Prioritise your health,
And push your Doctor for tests, too.

Something is happening.
That is becoming clear to me.
Is it life shattering?
For I'm just not how I should be.

Pill Rolling

Sat on the sofa.
Watching the tv.
Calmly relaxing.
Quite contentedly.

Nothing on my mind.
Feeling trouble free.
Started to chill out.
The best way to be.

Tremor in my hand.
It was plain to see.
My thumb and finger,
Like rolling a pea.

A twitch in my hand.
Then repeatedly,
Up into my arm,
Spasmodically.

What the heck is this?
It seemed odd to me.
My first feeling was,
Curiosity.

It happened at night,
While comfortably,
I would be at rest.
No activity.

My face was a mask.
Quite potentially,
Other symptoms, too,
Might come to plague me.

So this was the year,
Life revealed its fee.
Waiting patiently.
What would my fate be?

PART TWO
Diagnosis

I look back on that day, June 27th 2017, as the first day of the rest of my life. I reached a landmark that had been a very long time coming. I had arrived at Ipswich Hospital in readiness for an appointment with a neurologist. As I parked my car, I told myself that this surely had to be the day when I would get to find out what has caused me a lifetime of health problems and difficult symptoms.

I put my Blue Disabled Badge on the dashboard of my car. I made my usual careful swing and hoist out of my car and I reached for my trusty walking stick. I thought about how, with so much disability, I still have not achieved a full and clear diagnosis. I had even been previously mis-diagnosed with Fibromyalgia. It's been a lifetime of trying to find an explanation for my health issues. I felt the stress increase within me as my frustration and desperate search for a diagnosis welled up inside. "I've had enough", I thought. "I want this constant testing to be over with, once and for all."

I took a deep breath and I began my slow walk to the hospital entrance. Walking was a challenge. My mobility had deteriorated so much within the past several months. My right side of my body was hard to control and so I dragged my right leg, as I walked. I had to slow down and even stop at points along the path to the hospital entrance, just to recoup some of my energy and to minimise the increasing and painful discomfort.

Again, the incredulity hit me of how I could still be seeking a diagnosis with so many debilitating symptoms playing out. My right hand was twitching now that I was no longer holding the car steering wheel. It always seemed to twitch when resting after an activity.

What nobody would see was the relentless sensation of an inner vibration. It is a bizarre rhythmic sensation, deep within. As I entered the building, I wondered about how I would later be emerging from it, following my appointment? Would I have any definitive news?

I registered at Reception and was directed to the clinic I was to attend. I was booked in to meet a neurologist who leads the Parkinson's services. A man of very good reputation, by the name of Dr. Timothy Lockington.

I arrived in the waiting room, where a bright wall hanging tv screen featured the tv show 'Escape to the Country'. Ironically, the show that used to represent my dream of leaving London for a life in a rural country village by the sea. My husband and I had made this move back in 2007. It has been the best decision we ever made.

I looked around the waiting room, only to find that the other patients all appeared to be over 75 years of age. I was alerted to their twitching, shaking and stooped gaits and I felt a massive wave of nausea hit me like a locomotive. Apart from the guilt I felt at my reaction to these poor, lovely folk, I was hit by a major reality check; I saw myself in them. I recognised amplified versions of my own symptoms and I felt utter terror. I knew for sure what I had long suspected. Suddenly, the idea of going in to meet Dr. Lockington left me battling the urge to get the hell out of there and go home, as if this was something that I could hide from.

I calmed myself. I knew that I needed answers and I had come so far to reach this point. A nurse appeared. She called my name and asked if it was okay to weigh me and take my blood pressure. I joked, in front of everyone, that it is never okay to weigh me! She gently escorted me to a brightly lit room, with light yellow painted walls, in which a very wide chair was literally the weighing scales. She took my jacket and asked me to sit.

I struggled to get into this oddly shaped chair, with it's white metal arms and foot rests. The nurse set about recording my weight and taking my blood pressure; both of which were higher than I would have liked. I cracked a joke about my weight and I made another quip about my high blood pressure being due to my sudden terror! Then, back to the waiting area I trundled, to watch yet more clips of rural heaven on daytime television.

Soon my allotted number, that I had been clutching on a now crumpled ticket in my sweaty palm, appeared on the screen and from around the corner a middle-aged man appeared. He looked exactly as all neurologists seem to look. He had the usual incredibly kind and reassuring countenance and suitable spectacles.

So began what became an hour and a half of reflecting over my years of symptoms along with observation of me and of my physical symptoms in the room. This gentleman was not the man I was booked to see, but he did the 'groundwork' before Dr. Lockington joined us. I felt at ease, despite my natural apprehension. I then found that I also warmed to Dr. Lockington, who was another man with a kind, face and suitable reading glasses. These two men were incredibly good at their work.

I continued to respond to symptom-based questions, tick box questions and anecdotal questions and focused on trying to control my hand; the twitching and pill-rolling movements made worse by my stressed and exhausted state. I was asked to write a paragraph, which turned out to be in the usual tiny, illegible state. I wrote something witty about the dullness of having to keep coming to hospital! These two talented men continued asking me deep and personal questions about everything. I largely managed to avoid going red in the face, at this point, which is good.

"I am going to speak of a word that is going to represent the changes you have experienced. Parkinson's. I could send you for a DAT scan, but I think my colleague will agree that, taking your very long history of this ordeal, a lifetime of tests, monitoring and what we have heard and seen today into account, I do not need to send you to Addenbrooke's Hospital to make my diagnosis. It is incredibly clear and already well evidenced. You have Young Onset Parkinson's Disease." I held my breath. "Yes, you finally have your diagnosis, Mr. Parsons. I am diagnosing you completely and conclusively. I am so very sorry that you have had to endure such a long wait for this moment."

I remember going red in the face at this point and welling up with tears. A palpable sense of relief hit and I sat in some sort of stillness, soaking this news up. In that moment, I recalled how actor Michael J. Fox described the moment he was given his diagnosis; from his autobiography. "This is my moment", I thought to myself while the neurologist outlined what Parkinson's Disease is. "This is what it is like, in my moment of being diagnosed." I kept thinking.

I was somehow detached from myself, yet fully aware and hearing everything being said to me. "This is what it is like to be diagnosed, finally", I thought. It was as if I was trying to communicate with Michal J. Fox by telepathy so that I was sharing my version of being diagnosed, in response to his. I wish I could meet him and to thank him for all he has done for people with Parkinson's. His public 'sharings' of his experiences, particularly in his autobiographies, have literally given me the fortitude to persevere, on so many levels.

I was somehow very calm, silent and detached. It felt a little as though time was standing still. "This is the moment I have been heading toward. This is what it feels like. This is the person who is telling me. This is the room that it is happening in. This is the day, today". I felt a panic! "What is the date? Oh my God, I need to know the date of 'The

Day' that this is happening. Why can't I remember the date?" I wondered as my mind went blank. I chuckled to myself at how silly that was, all the while listening to very kind men in front of me as they described the rest of my life.

The senior of the two men then began speaking again. "...and all going well, in terms of life expectancy, I'd say thirty years at best. Statistically, you can expect to live a minimum of seven years post diagnosis, an average of fifteen years and a maximum of approximately thirty years. Given your age and that this is Young Onset, some things are in your favour. Research is always advancing."

This was unexpected information and it caused me to take a sharp intake of breath, but I completely appreciated, and I was comforted by, Dr. Lockington's kind tone of voice, his sincerity and his caring demeanour.

After twenty minutes or so of further discussion and a plan for the next week; the first stage of my new treatment plan, I found myself making my unsteady walk along the corridor and out to my car. In my hand, I carried papers and leaflets in a very sweaty grasp. "I've got Parkinson's Disease" was a phrase I found myself repeating in my head. That, and the intermittent feeling of nausea that hit me every couple of minutes as reality started to hit home.

I reflected on just how wonderful our NHS is and how scandalous it is that our Conservative Government has left the NHS and it's incredible staff in such a desperate and unforgivable state of poverty and distress. That's not an uneducated statement, I am a former Specialist Services Team Leader within the NHS and a former Commissioner of health services. I state the fact of the matter.

I began the process of breaking the news to my spouse, family and friends. I remain deeply touched by everyone's kindness, love and support.

I Sacked My Doctor

Doctor, I still have a problem
With my brain.
Mr. Parsons, are you really
Back again?
Doctor I can't function right and
I'm in pain.
Mr. Parsons, it is low mood
You sustain.
Doctor, all you've earnt from me is
My disdain

Doctor, nice to meet you, please would
You help me?
Mr. Parsons we have read your
History.
Doctor, you see motor skills are
Failing me?
Mr. Parsons go to see
Neurology.

Doctor, I accept your help so
Thankfully.

It's neurological Doctor
I'm quite sure.
Yes but, Mr. Parsons, we must
Test you more.
But really Doctor, this is now
Such a chore.
Patience, Mr. Parsons, we must
Reach the core.
Doctor, this must be the last time
I implore.

Doctor, I've been tested and scanned
As you know.
Mr. Parsons, this process is
Very slow.
But Doctor how much more must I
Undergo?
Mr. Parsons, some symptoms take
Years to show.

Doctor, these tests are becoming
My worst foe.

It's been years now, Doctor, what is
this about?
Mr. Parsons, the fibro is
now ruled out.
Your last Doctor mis-diagnosed
Causing doubt.
Mr. Parsons, we promise to
work this out.

Diagnosis Corrected

The sensibilities of being excited.
This uncompromising illness leaves me
blighted.
Yet to attain certainty made me
delighted.
The irony of this joy that's now
requited.

Astoundingly, painful truth is more
appealing.
For the first time, I could understand
my feelings.
If I burden others, that will leave me
reeling.
Bizarrely, this has been relationship
sealing.

Like true pilgrims we'd traversed the
path united.
My mis-diagnosis caused by the short-
sighted.
That misdemeanour eventually righted.
My consternation for those who left me
slighted.

So then came the time to disclose the
revision.
That Parkinson's was the source of the
rescission.
My fear was of scrutiny as an incision.
Yet for correction, we had all made
provision.

With my former diagnosis extradited.
Armed with the truth that my search
had expedited.
Disclosure would be like attention
invited.
I'll never forget the kindness this
ignited.

Sonnet for the Actor

You have become a brother in my heart.
Through time travel, you became
known to me.
Off screen is where you play your
greatest part.
You lead the way and teach me how to
be.

I read the words you wrote about your
life.
You described me within each heartfelt
line.
As you disclosed your symptoms and
your strife,
I recognised that you had described
mine.
From that key point my destiny was
clear.
The road ahead would be a bumpy ride.

With gratitude I hold your words so
dear.
Parkinson's brothers, walking side by
side.

Your gift has been to shine your light so
bright.
You give me hope that I may win this
fight.

Yes, You Can Do This

When life does not go your way.
When your world falls apart.
When your outlook is grey.
Yes, you can do this.

When trouble lurks at your door.
When there's no way forward.
When the outcome looks poor.
Yes, you can do this.

When your self-belief is low.
When there's no solution.
When there's nowhere to go.
Yes, you can do this.

When you have been rejected.
When you feel all alone.
When you feel neglected.
Yes, you can do this.

When you feel the pain of loss.
When your dreams are shattered.
When you don't give a toss.
Yes, you can do this.

When you feel completely lost.
When you don't know which way.
When the warmth turns to frost.
Yes, you can do this.

For all that you are inside.
For all that lies ahead.
Good days will calm the tide.
Yes, you can do this.

PART THREE

Progression

My phone alarm goes off at 6.45am, every day; it's time to take my medication.

This week, the sultry, velvet voice of Ella Fitzgerald singing 'Summertime', in a duet with the magical Louis Armstrong, has been my favourite way for the start of each new day to be announced. The delight of hearing the voices of these legendary performers initially fills my mind with joy and I forget. I forget that I have Parkinson's.

I smile as I hear Ella's soulful rendition that summertime is a time of easy living. Well, I'm looking forward to summer, in that case. Then, I try to move my body. I remember.

Outside, I can hear the birds singing and chirping their vibrant chatter. It's just a 'normal' day, right? What is 'normal', though? I look 'normal'. Yet, my muscles are tight and cramping, my hands pained and then begins the almost invisible spasm of arm muscles. My right leg, right shoulder and into the right side of my neck are all tight as if in great tension at the apprehension of a new day. Pain.

Sometimes my neck and shoulder muscles are set rigid, like concrete. My right foot is sometimes jolted into a cramp as soon as I move it. My face becomes the expressionless observation post from which I witness the sun shining into the bedroom; hope being delivered by natures light.

I am quiet. I am used to this now. I always chuckle to myself, even if I feel overwhelmed by the effort. I somehow manage to swing myself up and round to a sitting position, working my body into gentle stretching in readiness for reaching for my water and medication.

Pain and difficulty. My main task is not to drop my glass of water. Mission accomplished. I lay down, somewhat ungracefully, trying to ignore the back pain and I manage to return to sleep, even though my face is stuck in a slight grimace that I cannot ease until my medication begins its magic and kicks in.

My alarm goes off again. Ella is back. She croons a beautiful song; 'Fly Me to the Moon'. This reminds me to get out of bed, for 'normal' people are already up and about. A little later, in *my* version of a 'normal morning', I manage to slowly make my way downstairs like an aged chimpanzee. There is no elegance in the morning.

I reach the kitchen. I aim for a glass of water and, by this time, my next dose of medication. Tiring. I let our excited dogs out into the garden and I make my own bathroom pit-stop, as my medication continues to take effect. I battle the lingering tiredness as I awaken more fully. Our dogs head back to their beds until I can give them their breakfast.

With our bathroom downstairs, I immediately draw a hot bath; the main remedy for my cramping muscles and painful lower back. Bliss. Sometimes I cannot use the bath so, I shower.

Sometimes I cannot shower so, I use the bath. Sometimes I cannot use the bath or shower so, I wash. These are the decisions that must be made. I make them cautiously, for I have learnt several times the pain of falling down in the bathroom. Once washed and then dry, I set about the ridiculous, long and complex act of getting dressed into my clothes. All this effort and difficulty, before I even go about my day.

I go about my days. I go about my weeks and my months. I have, at the time of completing this small book, already gone about my life as a person with Parkinson's for two years since diagnosis. Parkinson's has been very busy during these two years. This has been a busy time for me, too; learning to accept that I am stuck with this illness for the rest of my days and doing all that I can to understand it and to better adapt to it. That is a journey that continues. It is a journey that involves me, my husband, my mother, my family, my friends and even my community around my home and my work.

The disease is progressing at a pace. I generally go about my life in peaceful acceptance and focusing on adapting and on enjoying life as fully as I am able. There are times, however, when the full scope of this debilitating disease hits me. I now truly know fear. I now also, even more than ever before, know the value of the meaningful things in my life and in our world.

This first two years has taught me that value of relationships with those closest to me and I have come to know and understand myself to a depth that I am truly grateful for, despite the illness.

There are many tough moments. There are many bad days. There are so very many challenges within each new day. I have had to learn that I am ill, that my illness causes me disability and that it will only get worse. I will never get better. That, above all else, has been the hardest and most challenging truth to face and nobody can ever know how utterly brutal and heartbreaking that simple truth is, to face, unless you have to face this inescapable truth yourself.

To know that it only gets worse. To know that I will only decline. I pray for a cure, in order that future generations will be spared this horror.

In spite of this harsh new reality, I

manage to retain my happiness. Life is beautiful. Our world is beautiful and even though I have more hardship ahead of me, I am grateful that I am here to be part of our crazy, beautiful world.

I owe a debt to my husband and all of those who are close to me, for their love and support; past, present and future. I owe much gratitude to the medical profession and the many medical staff who have supported me since I first presented, in childhood, with symptoms that, only recently, we have fully started to understand and make fuller sense of.

What I have yet to make sense of, is who I will yet become. My idea of older age was to hopefully still be physically well; agile, active and able to walk and to participate in anything that I set my mind to. I saw a more sophisticated older age and a gentlemanly disposition. Now, I have to consider that older age will be about contentment. It will be about finding simple joys. It will be about recognizing limitations and letting go of some of the dreams and aspirations. It will be about declining health; physically and mentally.

I comfort myself by saying that, at some point, this is what happens to us all in older age. The part I have to accept is that this process has already manifested itself in my middle-aged life.

On one hand, that causes me some resentment. I fully own that. On the other, I can see the enormous benefit of valuing the simpler things in life. I can see that by adapting now, I am going to do better as an older person with a chronic degenerative disease.

My word of wisdom to you all, should you share my misfortune, is to focus on what you can do, not that which you cannot do. This simple rule will preserve your emotional well-being and it will put you in a position of empowerment; always.

It is when people fall into making comparisons between who they are today, versus who they used to be, that the shadow of depression may appear. It is when people describe a future that they expected, and now feel denied, that resentment will open the door to that shadow of depression and welcome it in.

Why do some people complain that a certain type of expected future has been stolen from them? Has it been? Could it be? Isn't the future simply yet to be written? Are we not simply being who we are supposed to be and living out the story of our lives? I think so.

Unless your Parkinson's has been definitively caused by some pollutant, then it may just be that you were always going to be a person with Parkinson's. This is your story. In fact, even if you have been subject to a pollutant which has caused the disease, like it or not this is indeed now your story, too. Make good decisions. Live well.

Here's the deal:
Make your story a good one.

Parkinson's Pernicious Plan

Parkinson's appears impolitely.
It permeates within a person.
Pervading purposefully inside.
Its pernicious plan is palpable.
It perplexes and pains with aplomb.

This disease is dastardly and dire.
Its duty is to disrupt each day.
Devoutly it demands dopamine.
It desires to demean and destroy.
It diminishes and defeats us.

It affects our family and friends.
We fear the finality of it.
It is a fiendishly fickle foe.
Frequently, it falsely befriends us.
It fights our flaws so we may flounder.

Yet, suffering, we still soldier on.
Seeking some semblance of inner strength.
By showing steel and sardonic wit,
We somehow survive to stave it off.
This sad scene is set to strike again.

For Sure A Cure

Last night I compiled my weekly pills,
These chemicals that stave off my ills.
In their dosset looking just like sweets,
I guess in some way they are my treats.
For without my meds my symptoms
flare,
To go without them, I cannot dare.

My meds ensure that I move and speak,
They stop me twitching and help me
sleep.
Without them I would be unable,
And that would render me disabled.
I am so grateful for my healthcare,
I don't take for granted that it's there.

We must hope that there will be a cure,
That it will happen, I am quite sure.
Since many are diagnosed each day,
We must support them and show the

way.
We need more funding towards our
plight,
Researchers say the end's within sight.

Groundhog Week

Monday.

The sunlight.
My eyes blink.
Body tight.
My mind thinks.
Start the fight.
My heart sinks.
Meds alright.
With a drink.
Will feel right.
See the link.
Heal my plight.
Far from brink.
Rid the white.
Become pink.
Fly a kite.
Weakest link.
Ice and bite.
Cracks the rink.

Tuesday.

The sunlight.
My eyes blink.
Body tight.
My mind thinks.
Start the fight.
My heart sinks.
Meds alright.
With a drink.
Will feel right.
See the link.
Heal my plight.
Far from brink.
Rid the white.
Become pink.
Fly a kite.
Weakest link.
Ice and bite.
Cracks the rink.

Wednesday.

The sunlight.
My eyes blink.
Body tight.
My mind thinks.
Start the fight.
My heart sinks.
Meds alright.
With a drink.
Will feel right.
See the link.
Heal my plight.
Far from brink.
Rid the white.
Become pink.
Fly a kite.
Weakest link.
Ice and Bite.
Cracks the rink.

Thursday.

The sunlight.
My eyes blink.
Body tight.
My mind thinks.
Start the fight.
My heart sinks.
Meds alright.
With a drink.
Will feel right.
See the link.
Heal my plight.
Far from brink.
Rid the white.
Become pink.
Fly a kite.
Weakest link.
Ice and bite.
Cracks the rink.

Friday.

The sunlight.
My eyes blink.
Body tight.
My mind thinks.
Start the fight.
My heart sinks.
Meds alright.
With a drink.
Will feel right.
See the link.
Heal my plight.
Far from brink.
Rid the white.
Become pink.
Fly a kite.
Weakest link.
Ice and bite.
Cracks the rink.

Saturday.

The sunlight.
My eyes blink.
Body tight.
My mind thinks.
Start the fight.
My heart sinks.
Meds alright.
With a drink.
Will feel right.
See the link.
Heal my plight.
Far from brink.
Rid the white.
Become pink.
Fly a kite.
Weakest link.
Ice and bite.
Cracks the rink.

Sunday.

The sunlight.
My eyes blink.
Body tight.
My mind thinks.
Start the fight.
My heart sinks.
Meds alright.
With a drink.
Will feel right.
See the link.
Heal my plight.
Far from brink.
Rid the white.
Become pink.
Fly a kite.
Weakest link.
Ice and bite.
Cracks the rink.

What Time Cannot Heal

I was oblivious to time.
A ticking clock would be sublime.
Nowadays, I must pace myself.
Move time down to a lower shelf.
For time feels out of reach for me
The clock eludes me, constantly.

Doctors insist that I must rest.
Restorative time is what's best
But frankly that drives me crazy
That feels just like being lazy
There are many things on my list
I begrudge time already missed.

I need to be a busy bee.
There's always some activity.
I write, I work, I putter, too.
To me this recharging is new.
But it makes sense to take a break,
To prevent rigidity and shakes.

The challenge of becoming ill,
Requires of me my strength and will.
The tasks that I want to complete,
With Parkinson's they must compete.
Sometimes it seems such a fable.
Then I find that I'm disabled.

With all my plans for life ahead,
I now plan time to be in bed.
Then recharged I can carry on,
And not feel that resting is wrong.
My inner conflict is the key,
To living life contentedly.

Sonnet for my Husband

Before, my life was rudimentary.
Deep within, I knew that you existed.
Now, it's been quarter of a century,
Our connection could not be resisted.

Our union has always felt like fate.
Respected by our family and friends.
Our approach is not to leave things too
late.
Reinvention on which our life depends.
Shared adventures and travel far away,
You are my best friend, my life and my
light.
It saddens me that now within each day,
Parkinson's Disease has become our
plight.

Our nature through adversity is growth.
I love you and I am proud of us both.

The Maternal Plays Out

Mum:
I've decided that you cannot do,
The very things that I need of you,
And I will not choose to put you
through,
You helping me, for that might hurt
you.

Me:
This must stop for I need you to see,
When I help you it makes me happy.
It's the only way for me to be.
Your care creates disability.

Mum:
I know you want to do what is right.
You try to help me with my own plight.
Like me you also find life a fight.
But you must only rest, in my sight.

Me:
I know you mean well but it's not fair,
When I can see you need help right
there.
I'll do what I can because I care.
Only I decide what I can bear.

Mum:
I hear you and I will do my best.
Just please agree that you will take rest,
For watching you struggle is my test.
I need to provide you a safe nest.

Me:
But I have to do this for myself.
I now manage my declining health.
Your concern for me means all the
wealth.
Now please put your fears upon the
shelf.

Lighten Up

Sometimes things cause me to
reminisce,
Over the past and the me, I miss
Some people say ignorance is bliss.
I did not know I could feel like this.

There are mountains to climb in each
day,
And few directions to find my way.
When my symptoms just decide to stay,
And the bright sun is replaced by grey.

Sometimes a photo of me before,
Takes me back to when I could do more.
Right now it's easy to find a flaw,
And believe that I am life's short straw.

Yet no matter how tough life can be,
There's a light that shines eternally.
Alight within all humanity,
It provides hope for you and for me.

So on days when all you feel is pain,
When it seems your efforts are in vain,
When Parkinson's punches you again,
Look to the light and forego disdain.

Generations.

Spring's vibrancy shines.
Life abundant and renewed.
My slowness exposed.

Some People, As I

Before you read this poem:
You can read this poem down.
You can read it across the next page.
You can read it right page first.
You can read diagonals; page to page.

Some People, As I

Some people stand by me
Some people help me see
Some people hold my hand
Some people with me stand

Some people do not stay
Some people turn away
Some people seem to hide
Some people have not tried

Some People, As I

Before you read this poem:
You can read this poem down.
You can read it from the left page.
You can read it right page first
You can read diagonals; page to page.

Some People, As I

As I live with illness
As I go through decline
As I suffer symptoms
As I struggle to climb

As I fight to survive
As I try hard to thrive
As I face the bad days
As I try to stay alive.

Guilt

Dire lurch within my stomach's pit.
Parkinson's wields another hit.
I perceive that I am reeling,
From this foe with which I'm dealing.
Yet, I discern I must face more,
Of this disease that I deplore.

The future appears doomed and bleak.
Have I now summited life's peak?
My spouse and I have plans ahead.
Distant lands upon which to tread.
Foreboding thoughts of dreams taken.
Aspirations now forsaken.

I feel I've perpetrated crime.
My spouse now shares this pantomime.
Perhaps I should be convicted,
For the confines I've inflicted?
But the future remains untold.
We'll retain hope, as it unfolds.

We have already learnt to share,
Whatever cross that we must bear.
We adapt as we walk the path,
And we fill life with fun and laughs.
With some dreams already in place,
I think we're ahead of the race.

The future is not set in stone.
There'll be no joy if we bemoan.
As research makes progress each year,
They may resolve the things we fear.
Pursue the things while you're able.
Gather friends around life's table.

My Brave Friend

I have a friend who has PD.
His body shakes so constantly.
I feel he has it worse than me.
His bravery is plain to see.

I feel a fraud without such shakes.
Ashamed of any fuss I make.
His body suffers seismic quakes.
I admire him for all he takes.

My friend is young to suffer so.
Yet he's full of 'get up and go'.
I'd like to spare him from this woe.
His DBS is due soon, though.

This guy's as busy as a bee.
Central to his community.
Provider for his family.
The proudest dad you'd ever see.

My friend's self-doubt was just not
right.
This sincere man with pluck and fight.
I told him that his light shines bright.
Our hope for him soars like a kite.

With brain surgery very near.
You'd understand he has some fear.
I wish him all of life's good cheer.
By many folks, he is held dear.

....

Dedicated to my friend, Brendan Quinn.
A bravery of spirit I have rarely seen in
any person. It is my privilege to call
him my friend.

A Conservative Error

To our Tory PM, with dismay.
I find myself wracked with disgust.
Your team's letter arrived here today.
The contents are simply unjust.

Your Government must simply not
know,
Parkinson's Disease has no cure.
Many symptoms are hidden from show.
Each day is a trial to endure.

My neurologist saw me last week.
He assessed my symptoms with skill.
He observed my movement and my
speech.
Examples of how I am ill.

My partner joined the consultation.
For Care-Givers share this despair.
I recounted with trepidation,
Of the day I fell down the stairs.

Your PIP team has asked me to attend,
Their assessment where I must prove,
That my symptoms are real, not
pretend,
Despite how I struggle to move.

I may dribble or slur when I speak.
Sometimes I twitch, tremor or freeze.
I may need an unexpected leak!
I may fall on my bum, back or knees.

I may sleep at the drop of a hat,
Though seldom when I'm in my bed.
Hellish migraines that hit like a bat.
It's the pain and vomit I dread.

I scuff my boots, so I must buy more.
Only sometimes I prepare food.
Crockery that I drop to the floor.
I fall in the bathroom, while nude.

Confusion with my medication.
Unable to easily dress.
Repeated bouts of constipation.
My social life has become less.

My symptoms and pain are relentless.
Now a beard, for I cannot shave.
Reducing work, so now I earn less.
Occasional thoughts of my grave.

With shopping far too heavy to lift.
My clothes rip when I bump a wall.
Some relationships now have a rift.
Self-confidence can become small.

My handwriting is now so unclear.
My voice often weak and quiet.
Muscle tension and cramping, severe.
Reflux, no matter the diet.

I can't drive far, for I have to rest.
Restless legs incessant with shocks.
A grabber for reaching things is best.
I struggle to put on my socks.

This list is not exhaustive, by far.
Yet I sit here, feeling perplexed.
Your team's letter cuts right to my heart.
To reassess me, makes me vexed.

Parkinson's Disease only declines.
I just become more disabled.
PIP assessments cost resource and time.
My disease must seem a fable?

Degraded and judged is how I feel.
While PIP seeks to prove I am well.
They don't accept Parkinson's is real.
The disabled are put through hell.

Known as the 'Nasty Party', you are.
In defence you say "We spend more."
Yet PIP is how low you set the bar,
The disabled have to endure.

This poem evidences my strife.
The Government must now decide,
While another will take their own life.
Since your policies just deride.

End PIP reassessment, I implore.
For Parkinson's gets no better.
End the judgement and shame you
cause.
Each time you send your PIP letter.

Soldiering On

Thief.

Energy Stealer.

Climate Control Redundant.

Hinges Burning on Fire.

The voice that whispers unheard.

Seemingly, a punch in the senses.

The ice statue blights the bold
progression.

In the depths lies a confusing faulty
compass.

Lightening shocks and fires the signal of
impending assault.

The mighty system twitches the rhythm of the faceless mask.

The Beast in possession of the key to perpetual solitary confinement.

The exhausted soldier battles with a dastardly fiend with shape shifting capabilities.

The pins and the needles of war trigger the potential for mass defeat.

If the great volcano erupts, then hope must yet survive the engulfing savage fallout.

Leaves and chemicals may weaken the enemy, but inner belief finds the door to peace.

The wounded soldier loses grip of normality and in fight or flight, faces a new tomorrow.

A Mother's Eyes

She tells me she prays for me each night.
She insists that I will be alright.
She believes a cure will end my plight.
You cannot hide the pain in a mother's
eyes.

She says it's unfair that I am ill.
She gives me her love and strength of
will.
She walks with me as I climb uphill.
You cannot hide the pain in a mother's
eyes.

She lifts me up when I feel disdain.
She holds my hand when I am in pain.
She points to the sun when I see rain.
You cannot hide the pain in a mother's
eyes.

She listens to what I need to tell.
She responds with the right words so
well.
She says there is hope beyond this hell.
You cannot hide the pain in a mother's
eyes.

She insists that I try to stay fit.
She says she's tried to make sense of it.
She says on down days I must use wit.
You cannot hide the pain in a mother's
eyes.

She admits that God must hear her plea.
She offered to bear my ills for me.
She is my amazing mum, you see.
You cannot hide the pain in a son's eyes.

Pace Yourself

But I have so much to do.
Pace yourself.
But I have places to go.
Pace yourself.
But I have people to see.
Pace yourself.

But I have dreams to fulfill.
Pace yourself.
But I have tasks to complete.
Pace yourself.
But I have races to run.
Pace yourself.

But I have to battle time.
Pace yourself.
But I have money to earn.
Pace yourself.
But I have friends to meet with.
Pace yourself.

But I have two dogs to walk.
Pace yourself.
But I have gardening, too!
Pace yourself.
But I have people to serve.
Pace yourself.

But I have a spouse to love.
Pace yourself.
But I have new things to learn.
Pace yourself.

But I'm going fucking mad!

Pace yourself.

Choosing Visibility

As a writer, I am used to ink.
This substance conveys the things I
think.
Both within a printer and a pen,
From the comfort of my writing den.

But today I will meet ink anew.
My thoughts drawn into my first tattoo.
There can be no progress without pain.
Symbolic meaning that is engraved.

It seems somewhat like a code to me.
My own hieroglyphs for all to see.
It represents all that makes me strong.
Which will motivate me to go on.

The tattoo will prompt dedication,
Not to forget my medication,
And it will show that there is no shame,
For Parkinson's Disease to be named.

In some ways just like being branded.
This honest mode for being candid.
The image enables all to see.
This major part of my life story.

Stuck Without Access

I appear to be stuck in a room.
Outside there is a village meeting.
I hear sounds of joy and groans of
gloom.
My chance to leave was only fleeting.

The villagers are gathered next door,
To discuss community issues.
My need for dinner grows ever more.
All I have are pens, pad and tissues.

You see I was here doing my job,
Counselling clients throughout the eve.
At home my dinner is on the hob,
Which is why I am ready to leave.

But I'm not one to disrupt debate.
It would be impolite and unkind.
I thought it better to go home late,
While villagers say what's on their
minds.

It now feels this meeting won't
conclude.
I am now starting to feel confined.
I'm sure they didn't mean to be rude.
Disabled access, not on their minds.

I was delighted to leave at last,
Though I cut through the last of their
talk.
Around tables and chairs I squeezed
past.
'Ditched my stick due to no space to
walk.

They did not mean to block, there's no
doubt.
With no space for my stick I could fall.
But I managed to get myself out.
There's a lesson here now for us all.

Be aware of how hard it can be,
When there's no space to walk with my
stick.
Disabled access must be kept free.
Please review this matter, very quick.

My Nemesis

Time to dream awhile.
Healing and recovery.
Yet sleep evades me.

Defiance

Confined by the failings of my brain.
Destined to decline, I fight in vain.
Sometimes I could scream but I refrain.
Each day challenges me once again.

I observe my health flow down the
drain.
There is no recovery to gain.
This cruel disease has earnt my disdain.
In my forties, I walk with a cane.

I had aspirations to attain.
With limitations that are now plain.
I still seek out sunshine in the rain.
Hopefulness is not a thing I feign.

Ahead lies much suffering and pain.
Yet belief in a cure, I sustain.
It's the optimism I retain,
That holds fear at bay and keeps me
sane.

No light at the end, for which to aim.
I play but I cannot win this game.
A broken dream would be much the
same.
I won't give in, I keep light aflame.

Confined by the failings of my brain.
Destined to decline, I fight in vain.
Sometimes I could scream but I refrain.
Each day challenges me once again.

Set Apart

Like the square peg in a round hole.
The black sheep or the broken bowl.
Like one mature student in the class.
The short straw or the 'Do Not Pass'.
Like the faded actor of prior fame.
The odd one out or the horse now lame.
Parkinson's sets you apart.

Like the fabled 'Man in the Moon'.
The 'unsinkable' Titanic or Brigadoon.
Like Marilyn Munster or the odd sock.
The ugly duckling or the faulty clock.
Like the mis-matched shade of paint on
the wall.
The out of tune singer or the class
know-it-all.
Parkinson's sets you apart.

But...

Like a mountain awaits for its peak to
be climbed.
The race to be won or a developing
mind.
Like buried treasure about to be found.
The piano concerto or the healed
wound, unbound.
Like the young bird's first flight from
the nest.
The conquering hero or doing our best.
'I' set Parkinson's apart.

Hope Grows

Determination is desired. Make a
decision.
Hope grows.
Open up to optimism. Oust obvious
doom.
Hope grows.

Feel the fortitude from within. Find
your foundation.
Hope grows.
Antipathy is no asset. Acceptance is all.
Hope grows.

Savour the simple, small things. Be
solutions focused.
Hope Grows.
Construct a community and live
creatively.
Hope grows.

Go green. Gardening grows gratitude
and gracefulness.
Hope grows.
Manage time. Truth; we have today.
Twenty four hours.
Hope grows.

Participate with people. Play. Party.
Plan good things.
Hope grows.
Together. Talking is treatment. Tell
people. Type it.
Hope grows.

Hang on to hopefulness. Hear your
happy inner voice.
Hope grows.
Sorrow makes sense but do not select
self-pity.
Hope Grows.

Ban belligerent behaviours and beliefs.
Cease blame.
Hope grows.
Engineer expectations that fit the
evolved you.
Hope grows.

Learn to love. Listen to your body.
Laugh the loudest.
Hope grows.
Study something. Create sanctuary.   Be
serene.
Hope grows.

Know your needs. Nurture the self.
Nourish healthy living.
Hope grows.
Contribute. Care for others.
Accomplish your cause.
Hope grows.

Welcome well-being. Think wisely.
Worry just wastes time.
Hope grows.
Help others. Hold those dear to you.
Hear your heart beating.
Hope grows.

Effort Ongoing

Bang, as the dystonia punches me.
Slam, as I cramp in my neck and my
arm.
Crunch, at the onset of rigidity.
Ouch, due to symptoms that inflict pain
and harm.

Zonk, though narcolepsy happens
rarely.
Blink, for insomnia causes dry eyes.
Count, for I can sleep but only barely.
Shout, when lucid dreaming makes me
arise.

Slur, despite trying so hard just to speak
Dab, if mouth's corner insists it will wet.
Gulp, for dry mouth makes oration so
weak.
Push, as words stick at face masking's
onset.

Trudge, as bradykinesia kicks in.
Reel, as 'wobbly' is the epithet used.
Still, while the ice sculpture form now
sets in.
Crash, but each fall leaves me feeling
abused.

Pinch, as each twitch and tremor
exhaust me.
Pull, for though weakened, I must still
get dressed.
Shake, when sometimes I carry my nice
tea.
Brace, for this is not the end of the test.

Two Years Since My Diagnosis

Change happening in innumerable
ways.
Medication doses segmenting my days.
Navigating life in a bit of a daze.
Two years since my diagnosis.

Pioneer of my destiny and prepared.
To do what I can even when I feel
scared.
With heartfelt gratitude for those who
have cared.
Two years since my diagnosis.

Sleep's allure is lost to me forever more.
Incredulity as more things seem a chore.
The slam of my body as I hit the floor.
Two years since my diagnosis.

I completed a course to change my
career.
'Take the bull by the horns'; removes
any fear.
My life as a therapist, I have held dear.
Two years since my diagnosis.

Adversity reveals its face unto me.
The shackles from which I seek my
liberty.
Revealing my symptoms in speech
therapy.
Two years since my diagnosis.

The human condition needs a
connection.
Failing on this would be an insurrection.
I have achieved a new social direction.
Two years since my diagnosis.

Prescriptions reveal the true state of decline.
Long gone are the days when I'd say "I feel fine."
Like being branded at that moment in time.
Two years since my diagnosis.

I am transitioning to be a writer.
I'm not giving up; I remain a fighter.
But this new career makes my future brighter.
Two years since my diagnosis.

The throes of progression across many years.
This heretic presence disrupts through dark fears.
The truculent gremlin grimaces and sneers.
Two years since my diagnosis.

Online I made friends, with Parkinson's Disease.
We designed a support group for those in need.
For my sense of purpose this planted a seed.
Two years since my diagnosis.

I do not walk this rutted road on my own.
My spouse, too, has seeds of purpose that he's sown.
It's clear that out of tribulation, we've grown.
Two years since my diagnosis.

PART FOUR

Walking Parkinson's Road

The day of the second anniversary of my diagnosis is now behind me. Although I believe that my symptoms of Parkinson's have been a part of my life, always, I feel that I have only truly started my relationship with Parkinson's since the day of my diagnosis. Prior to that, it was my belief that I had Parkinson's, but it remained an uncertainty in my life for so long. I had merely been on a quest for answers.

Today, Parkinson's and I have become well acquainted. We know each other well and we co-exist within my form. There is literally not an hour in my waking time that I do not think of it; not out of desire but out of necessity. Parkinson's impacts on every aspect of my life. The breadth of symptoms is staggering and the way in which this disease mocks and assaults is regularly shocking. I literally cannot know how I will be on any given day, until I am awake that morning and, even then, that can all change in a matter of time.

While I know that cell death in a region of my brain, called the substantia-nigra, is the direct cause of my symptom's, due to the diminishing ability to create dopamine, the certain cause for Parkinson's itself remains elusive. As this region of my brain dies, and I am told by my Neurologist that by now only up to 15% of this part of my brain is likely to be alive at best. This relentless dwindling will continue to diminish important aspects of me and my abilities over the next few years.

I am incredibly fortunate, in that I live within a society that has access to medication that helps my brain continue to receive the building blocks for dopamine, plus all of the supporting medications which go some way towards addressing the forty or so symptoms of Parkinson's.

While I still have some brain cells in the substantia-nigra region of my brain; the 15% or fewer that remain, I may still benefit from some use of the key medication for Parkinson's; Levodopa. This medication is the reason that I am largely able to move, to walk, to talk and to function. It feels like a miracle.

I am told that on average I should have three to seven years of a 'honeymoon' period of using Levodopa, before the percentage of cells that I still have become too few to make much effective use of it. When that time comes, a whole new set of change and challenge will become known to me.

I am also mindful that my Neurologist informed me, on the day of my diagnosis, that the average life span, currently, following diagnosis is a minimum of 7 years, an average of 15 years and a maximum of 30 years. I was relieved that, at least two years ago when diagnosed, my Neurologist felt that my opportunity for the maximum life span was pretty good. I may just make it into my seventies!

Two years have now passed, since diagnosis. Time flies!

One point I would like to make here, as a matter of awareness and consideration, is that the Parkinson's community, locally and globally, must look at how deaths are recorded. All too often I hear that Parkinson's is not a 'death sentence'. That, directly, may be true. Indirectly, however, I believe this may be inaccurate and presented in a way which minimises the risk of mortality in the minds of patients, medical professionals and society in general.

Many people with Parkinson's die from sustaining injury through falling or from infection; particularly pneumonia. There are a broad range of incidents or contributing factors to why a person with Parkinson's has passed away.

What needs to be considered is how the deaths are recorded. If we only record a death due to injury sustained through a fall, we may not be recording that the person only fell at all because they have Parkinson's. If we record pneumonia infection as cause of death, are we recording that this was ultimately a Parkinson's factor?

My recommendation is that this subject, of how the deaths of people with Parkinson's have been, and are, recorded, is revisited. I would like to know that when someone says 'Parkinson's is not fatal', that this is a known fact because we are including Parkinson's as the underlying cause for fatal infections and falls, for example. Only then will the true number of fatalities, attributable to Parkinson's, locally and globally be known and only then will appropriate funding for treatment and care be provided.

I would like to take this opportunity to thank all of the medical professionals who have supported and treated me over the years. In particular, I draw praise to Leiston Surgery, in Leiston here in the county of Suffolk. Without this exceptional team, here on the beautiful Suffolk coast, my diagnosis may never have happened. This accolade must go to Dr. Karen Blades, her Partners and their team. I thank you.

My Neurologist, Timothy Lockington, has informed me that he is due to retire imminently. I must take this opportunity to offer him my sincere thanks and heartfelt gratitude for his kindness, his support, his professionalism and his humanity. I could not have hoped for better care than has been afforded to me by him, and his team, at both Ipswich and Aldeburgh Community Hospitals, here in this beautiful county of Suffolk.

Everyone truly close to me, in my life, has remained utterly supportive, kind and helpful throughout my years of intense struggle while searching for the elusive cause of my symptoms. I cannot thank these members of my family, friends and community enough. I am humbled by such kindness and I continue to be. Thank you all.

That, along with the wonderful new friends in my life who also are living with, or are affected by, Parkinson's and who walk Parkinson's Road, too. We are making this journey together and, though we have already seen the tragic loss of some of those friends, our community is strong and united and full of fight, compassion and determination to push for better treatment and for a cure.

The key now is to live well, remain hopeful and to find new ways in which to thrive while experiencing the adversity that Parkinson's brings with it.

Look in the Right Place

We must look into the dark,
To find our might.

We must search inside our hearts,
To find what's right.

We must walk along the road,
To find our sight.

We must offer out our hand,
To find the light.

We must certainly look up,
To find the bright.

About the Author

Dean G. Parsons was born in the London Borough of Ealing. Dean was diagnosed with Parkinson's in June 2017 but he traces his symptoms back to early childhood and even further back into his maternal family line.

Dean lives in the English county of Suffolk; fulfilling a dream to live in an old country cottage, in a pretty village along one of England's beautiful coastline areas. After twenty years together, Dean and his partner, Kevin, married and they live happily with their two dogs.

Alongside their plentiful professional responsibilities, Dean and Kevin are both part of a voluntary team who run a global, free support group for people with Parkinson's and their loved ones. This Facebook based group has, at 2019, achieved a membership in the thousands, worldwide. It is called 'Parkinson's Road'.

Dean, a Diploma Qualified Writer, writes an already very successful blog at: www.deanparsons.net Dean has attracted well over thirty thousand readers to his blog, in the first three years since its inception in 2016. This number continues to grow, year by year.

Alongside this, Dean has achieved a nearly two decades long career as a Psychotherapist. Due to Parkinson's, Dean recognises that his work in this field will eventually move more to written publications, as his symptoms eventually prevent him from seeing clients in-person for courses of therapy.

Dean writes in a variety of genres and he has an Author Page on the web site of Amazon.

Dean is now a familiar voice as a guest presenter on Radio Parkies; an international radio service for the Parkinson's community. There, Dean has also read some of the poetry from this book and this has been very well received by listeners.

This book of poetry will be classed as 'Volume 1' in a series of autobiographical works that Dean will be producing over time.

Dean has campaigned throughout his life for equality rights, conservation, animal protection and he has served society, alongside his professional roles, with almost constant voluntary work since 1996.

"Thank you for taking an interest in my written work. I hope you find that my writing offers a meaningful and entertaining experience." – Dean G. Parsons.

Fin.